Stars

of the

Silver Screen

by

Shan Peck

Shan Peck

Copyright © 2018 Shan Peck

All rights reserved.

ISBN-13: 978 - 1728816272

DEDICATION

To everyone who loves art and movies.

Featured artists

JOHN CUNNANE - U.S.A.

RAMESH MAHALINGHAM - INDIA

STACY TAYLOR - TURKEY

BALAZS SEBOK - ITALY

FITZPATRICK JIM - U.S.A.

JANET LAVIDA - U.S.A.

DENISE FULMER - U.S.A.

WALTER ISRAEL - U.S.A.

Stars of the Silver Screen

Author

Janet Lavida was born in the Chicago suburbs and lived there for the better part of her life. Her love for art began in those formative years. No doubt the influence of her mother, having been an artist herself, this was the stepping stone that enhanced Lavida's love to become a giver.

'GIVERS' A painters brush, a composer's
notes, a poet's pen, all share in the opening up and the leading through countless corridors of a universe within an universe. For each grasps beyond the limitations of mere sight, sound, and understanding. The artistic reach extends between the real and the imagined. They have earned the art of constancy, by way of continually being. Their expression, be it either masqueraded before your face, echoed through your mind, or simply pressed across your heart, are the gifts from these givers. With clarity, they are but one language holding powers to cross all barriers. The artist is ageless and shows no favoritism to the young nor the old. The givers are timeless, for they are before, they are after, they are now, and thus, forever be they the always.
A 'Giver' among 'Givers'
In school Lavida's talents were first recognized. However, it was approximately at the age of twenty-five that she realized a fuller potential. It was then that she began to take art to a more professional level. Her enriched desire to paint began to intensify, and as she developed physically, mentally, and emotionally, she broadened her artistry to encompass the passionate world around her. Lavida is self-taught artist, using her own technique, which is her signature. Although, she has painted with water color, and acrylic, it has been her preference to use the oil medium. Yet, people most interested her. Lavida tries best to capture the essence of the individual and place it upon the canvas. She is not subject to doing only portraits, the animate and inanimate. Having placed her signature upon murals, canvas, book covers, and the like. She would like to broaden her field, to include you. Now if you would proceed.....

Stars of the Silver Screen

Terrence Howard – art by Janet Lavida

9.0 x 12.0 inches

Media - acrylic on canvas

$500.00

jlavida@aol.com

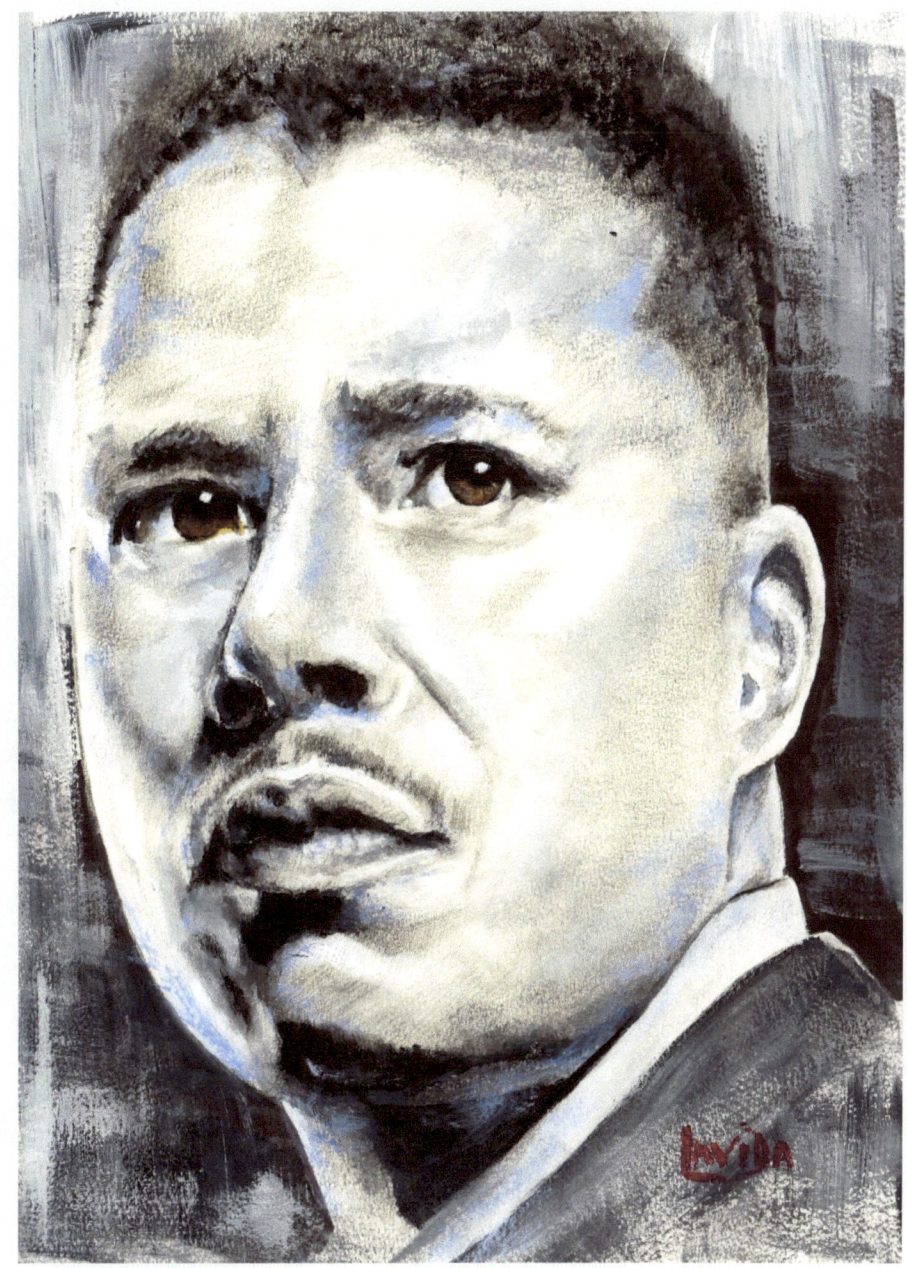

Leonardo DiCaprio – art by Janet Lavida

9.0 x 12.0 inches

Media - acrylic on canvas

$900.00

jlavida@aol.com

Stars of the Silver Screen

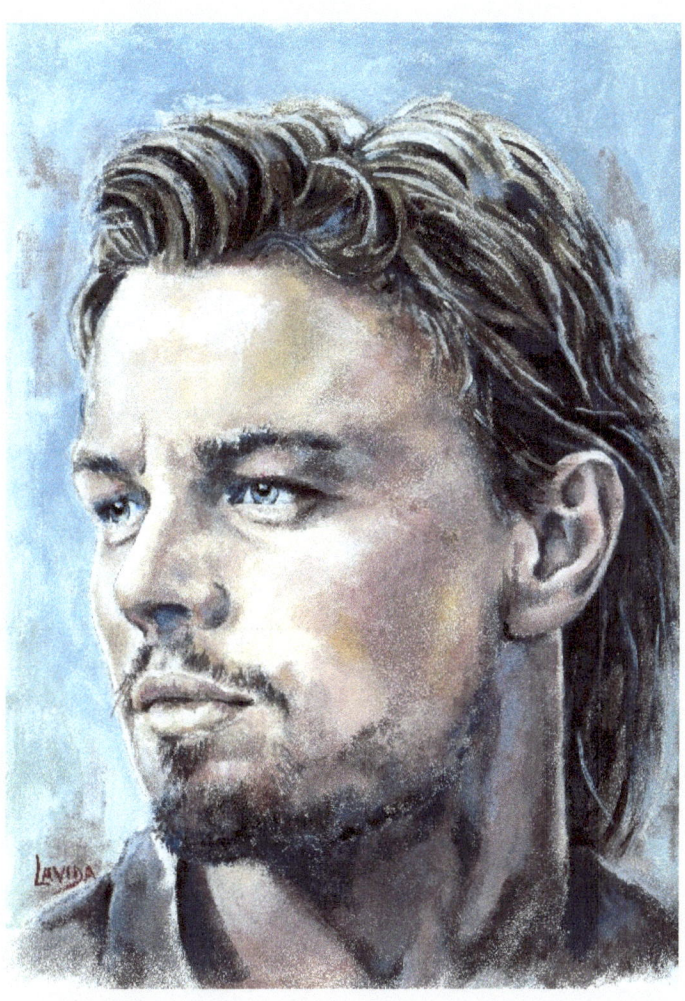

Johnny Depp – art by Janet Lavida

9.0 x 12.0 inches

Media - acrylic on canvas

$500.00

jlavida@aol.com

Stars of the Silver Screen

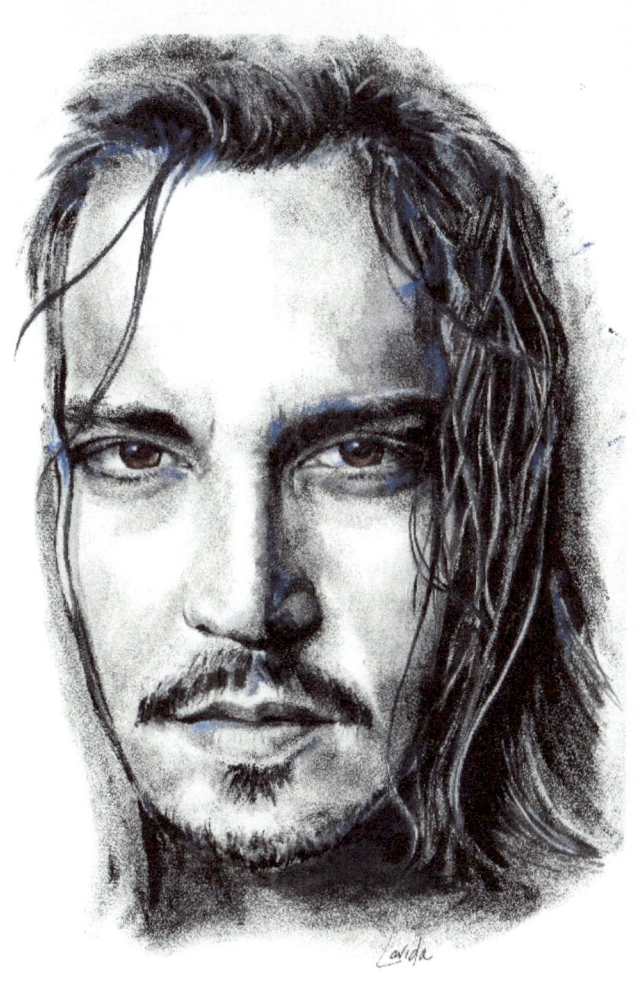

Author

Jim Fitzpatrick of the United States is a self-taught artist, photographer, former professional Roller Derby skater, retired fire fighter, portrays an eccentric butler character for a pro wrestler and a "Jack of All Trades".

Jim was selected as one of Art Tour International Magazine's Top 60 Master of Contemporary Art in 2014, 2015, 2016, 2017 and 2018. He was also selected by them as one of Art Tour Inter-national Magazine's Top 20 Fine Art Photographers for 2017! To date he has published 5 photo books and held 3 art exhibitions. At one he displayed his works of boxer Mike Tyson who was on hand. Some of Jim's works have been published in books, magazines, programs, on advertising posters, appeared on TV and on National Geographic's site. As someone who suffers from chronic pain he hopes to inspire other living with chronic pain.

Stars of the Silver Screen

LUCY LIU – ART BY JIM FITZPATRICK

15.0 x 20.0 inches

MEDIA - PENCIL / PASTELS, COLOR PENCILS AND CHARCOAL ON ARCHES WATERCOLOR PAPER

$1000,00

jim_f_94080@yahoo.com

Stars of the Silver Screen

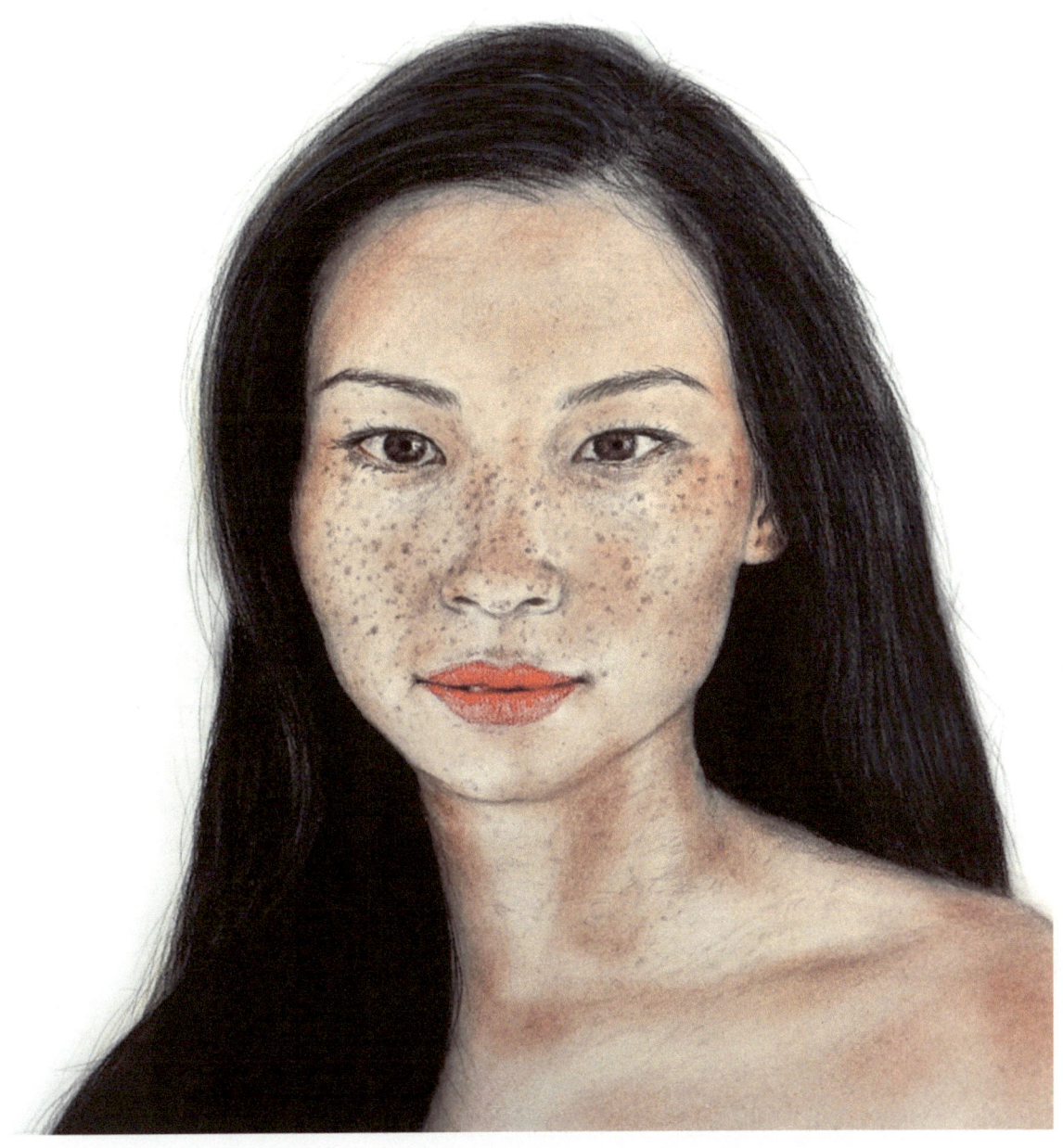

Author

Stacy Taylor lives and works in Turkey, where she has taught the English language since 2010 and has served as an instructor at the university level since 2013. A native of the U.S. from the state of Kansas, she spent her early years studying art and photography, culminating in a degree in Commercial and Advertising Arts from Salina Area Technical College. She has worked as a freelance artist on commission since 1998 and is fluent in all mediums — principally graphite, pastel, and colored pencil. Her illustrations comprise a versatile range of subjects, including landscapes, animals, automobiles, still life, and the human figure. For the past thirty years, she has pursued an interest in developing her technique toward the perfection of the human figure in realistic illustration portraits. She is a very detail oriented artist, creating hundreds of portraits over the years of exceptional quality. When not working on commission work she illustrates Hollywood Movie Stars or Famous people for practice and educational purposes. Her work has been publicly exhibited in such venues as the Saline Area Public Television Art Gallery (1998), and a special exhibition in Turkey, sponsored by Bir Medya and the Çorum Municipality (2017).

Visit her online portfolio at http://wwwstacybledsoe74.daportfolio.com. You can also visit her online page at https://www.facebook.com/atailoredimage (all links can be found on 'A Tailored Image by Stacy Bledsoe' Facebook page). If you wish to have a portrait done by Stacy, you must provide your own photograph. Feel free to contact her at the above sites or email her at bledsoe_stacy@yahoo.com, for available sizes, prices or any further questions

Stars of the Silver Screen

MORGAN FREEMAN – ART BY STACY TAYLOR

25.0 x 35.0 centimeters

MEDIA - PENCIL / GRAPHITE ON PAPER

$250.00

bledsoe_stacy@yahoo.com

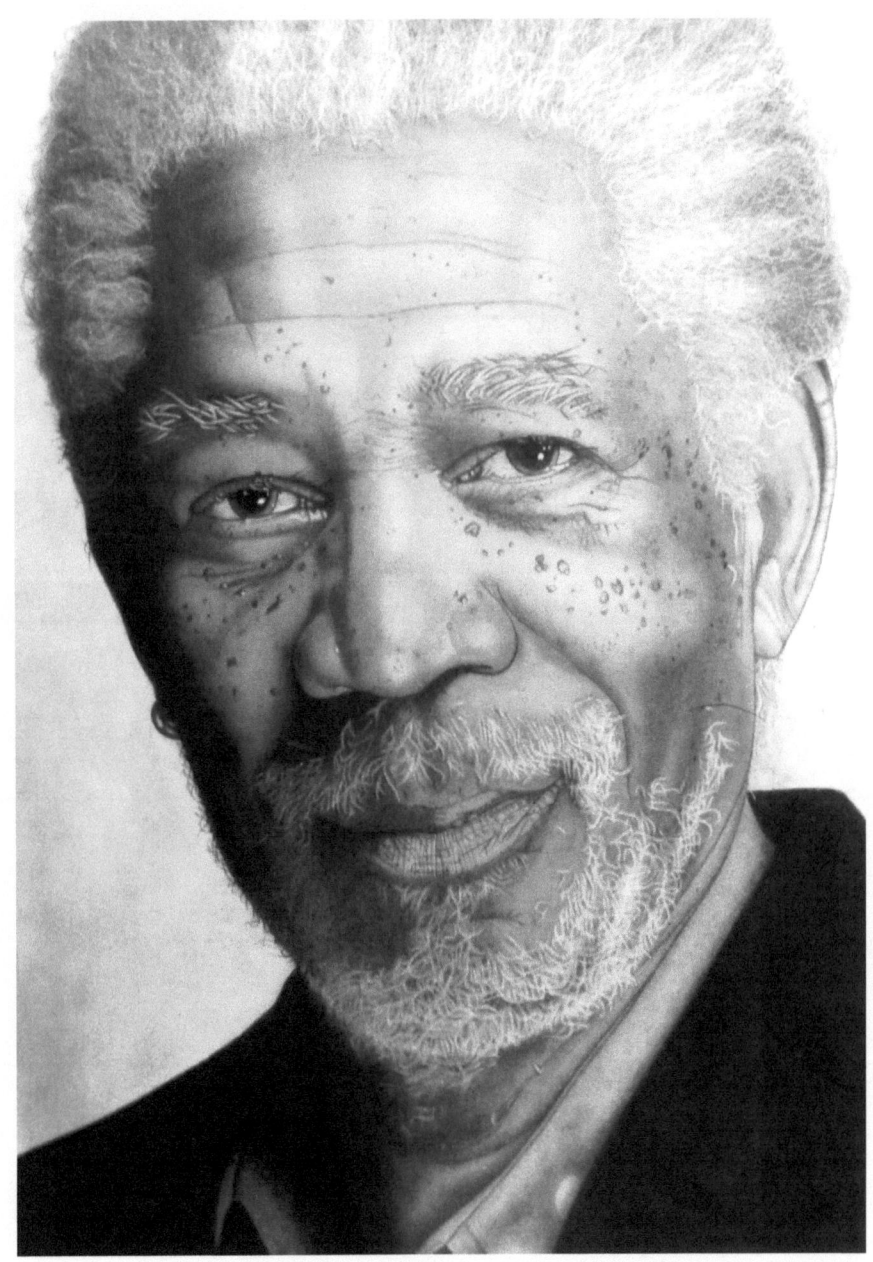

PAUL WALKER – ART BY STACY TAYLOR

25.0 x 35.0 centimeters

MEDIA - PENCIL / GRAPHITE ON PAPER

$250.00

bledsoe_stacy@yahoo.com

Stars of the Silver Screen

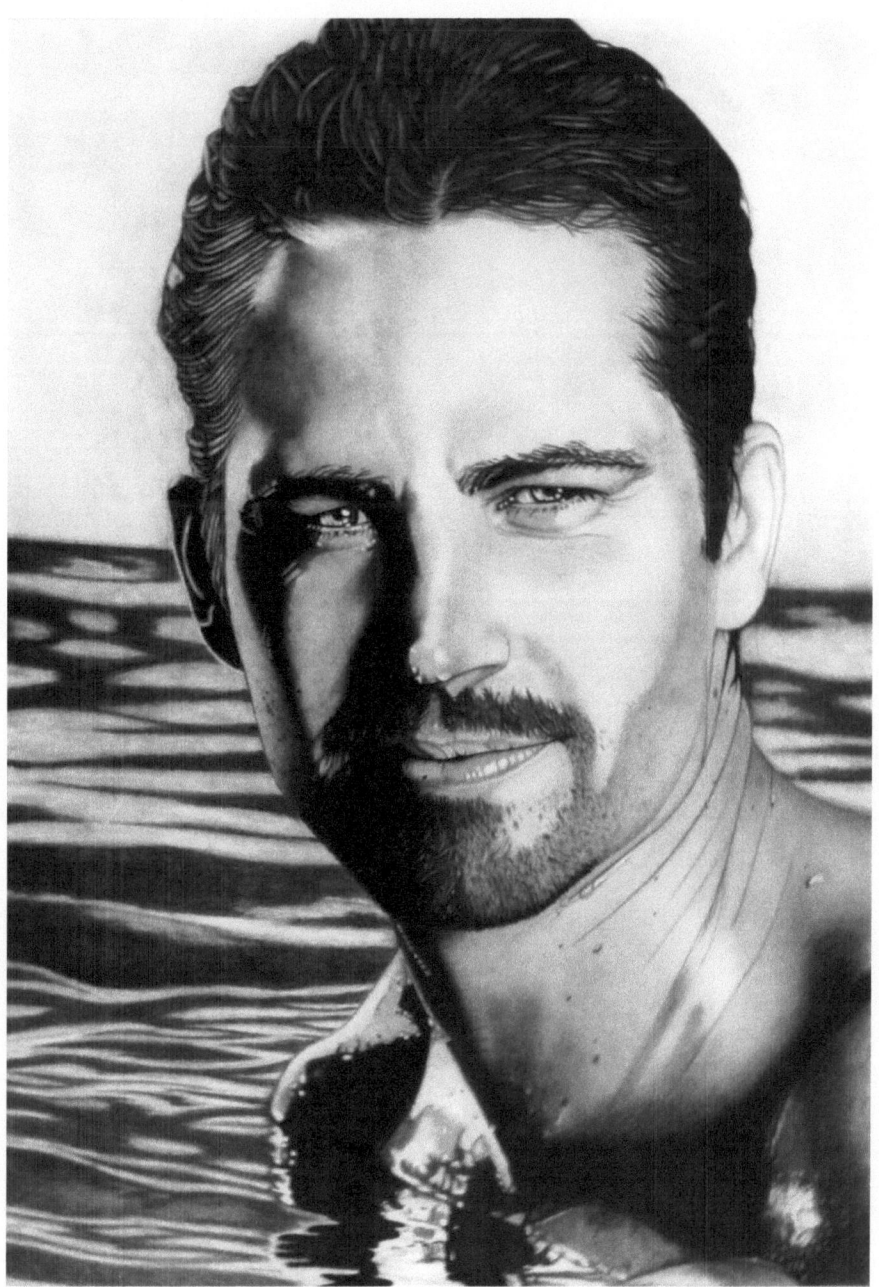

JOHNNY DEPP – ART BY STACY TAYLOR

31.0 x 50.0 centimeters

MEDIA - PENCIL / GRAPHITE ON PAPER

$350.00

bledsoe_stacy@yahoo.com

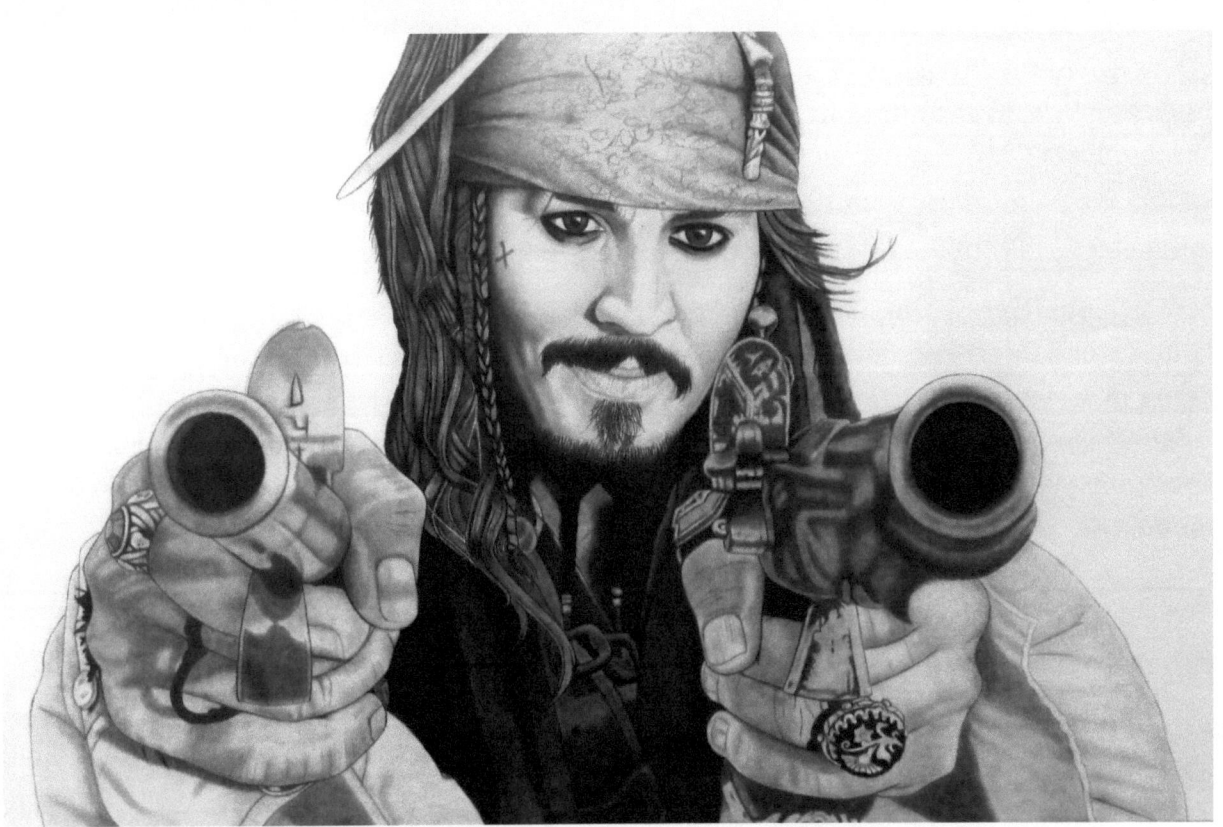

Author

Balazs Sebok was born in Hungary in 1982, nowadays he lives and works in Milan, Italy where the influence of any kind of different art is unquestionable, it's part of his everyday life, like exhibitions, art shows, street arts. He attended universities in Hungary and he is a Mechanical engineer and economist by profession and works in the financial area for more than 10 years but the interest in arts, especially for drawing, painting and photography is in his life since he was a child.

He is completely a self-starter, freelancer, hobby artist and for the past years, he has pursued an interest in developing his technique toward the perfection of the human figure in realistic illustration portraits. His illustrations comprise a versatile range of subjects including human portraits, landscapes, architectural structures, flowers and design of tattoos. His favorite artists and inspirations are Luis Royo, Boris Vallejo and Julie Bell, H.R. Giger, Diego Fazio, Robin Eley and Salvador Dali.

Stars of the Silver Screen

ROBERT DE NIRO – ART BY SEBOK BALASZ

29.7 x 42.0 centimeters

MEDIA - Graphite pencil on Fabriano paper

$500.00

balazs.sebok@outlook.com

Stars of the Silver Screen

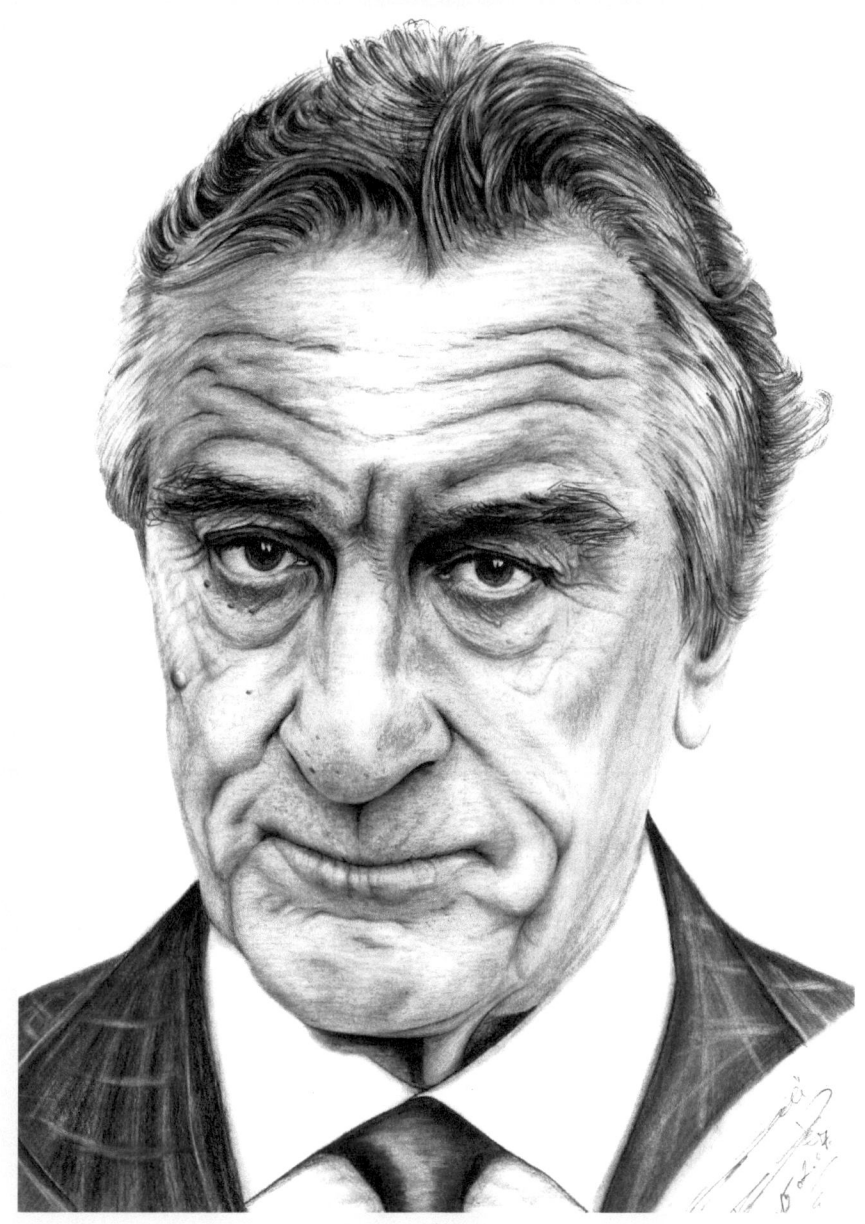

Author

Walter Israel is an artist working in graphite pencil and charcoal. He has a passion for drawing portraits of people and animals. Walter's working journey has taken him from a career spanning three decades in Germany as a graphic designer for renowned publishing companies to crossing the ocean to arrive on the shores of sunny Florida. His authentic inspiration for art includes the one of horsemanship. These powerful four-legged teachers continue to provide a distinct and profound roadmap to nature, as well as the dogs that now surround Walter at home which offer insightful life lessons from the canine perspective. The woman he married, dances with words, and her comments can perhaps best summarize his work: "It is such a joy to observe Walter transform a blank page into such memorable images. Combining a genuine connection with people and animals with such creative talent, he have autographed your masterpiece of life with excellence. "Walter Israel sell his Art through FineArtAmerica.com and his website: www.walterisrael.wixsite.com/fineart

Stars of the Silver Screen

HUGH JACKMAN – ART BY WALTER ISRAEL

11.0 x 14.0 inches

MEDIA - CHARCOAL ON PAPER

$950.00

walterisrael@web.de

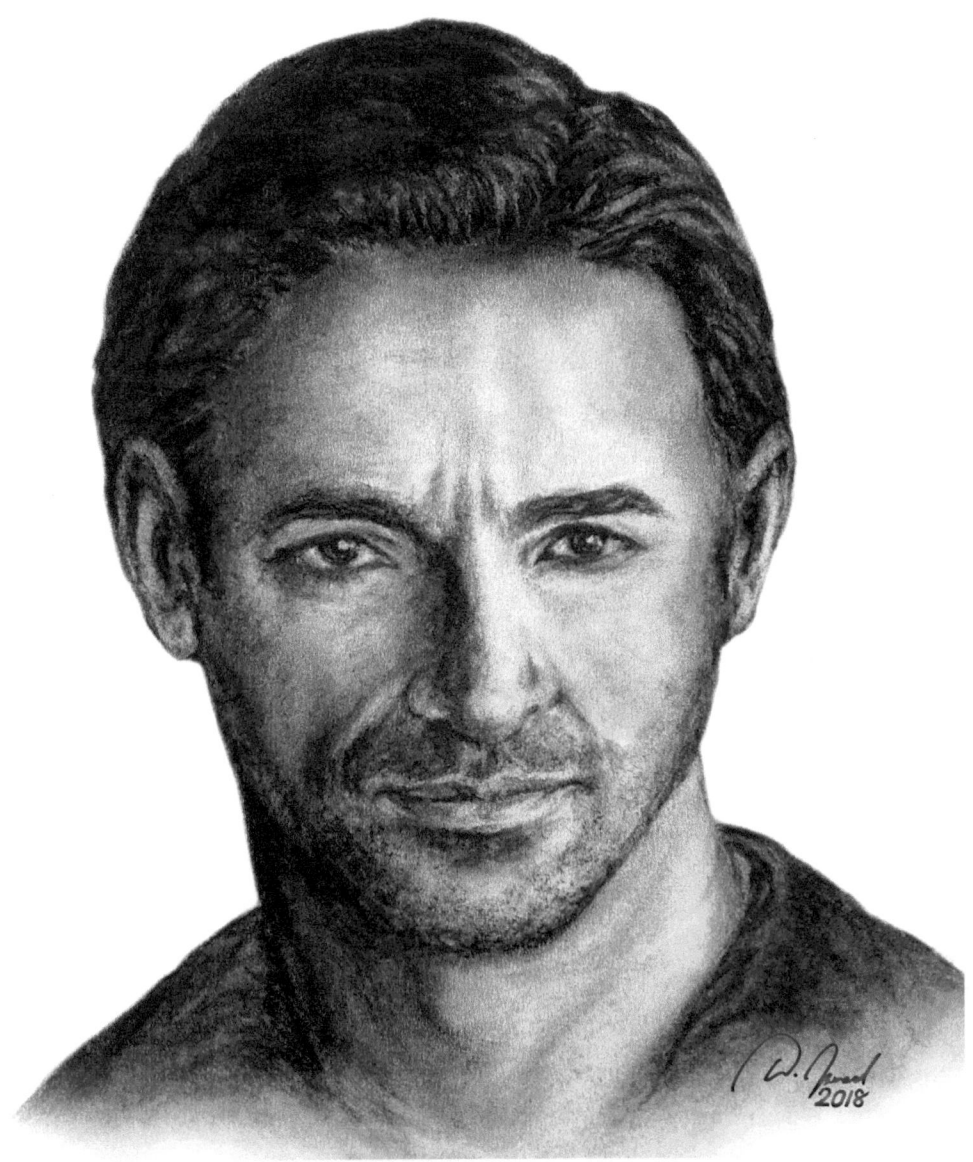

NICOLE KIDMAN – ART BY WALTER ISRAEL

11.0 x 14.0 inches

MEDIA - CHARCOAL ON PAPER

$550.00

walterisrael@web.de

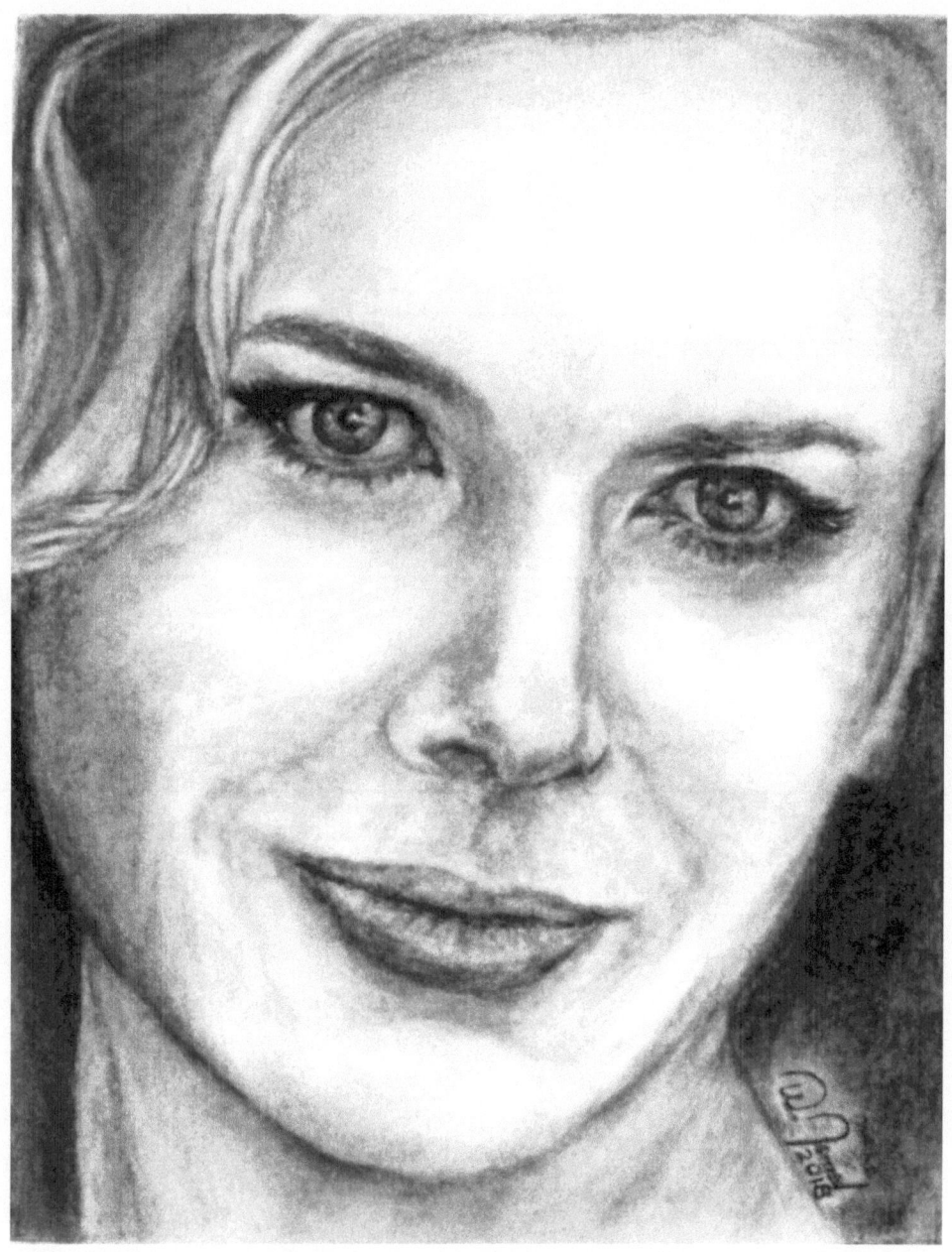

Author

Born in the Bronx, John Cunnane is a self-taught NY artist. He started painting in college but it wasn't until an early retirement from the corporate world that it became a full time passion. He embraces multiple styles to paint acrylic on canvas abstracts, semi-abstracts, landscapes, portraits and interpretive copies of famous art works. He describes himself as internally driven to add color to the world every day. He currently sells his art through Fine Art America and works as a portrait artist on a commission basis.

Stars of the Silver Screen

MARILYN MONROE – ART BY JOHN CUNANNE

8.0 x 10.0 inches

MEDIA - ACRYLIC ON CANVAS

$350.00

johncunanne@gmail.com

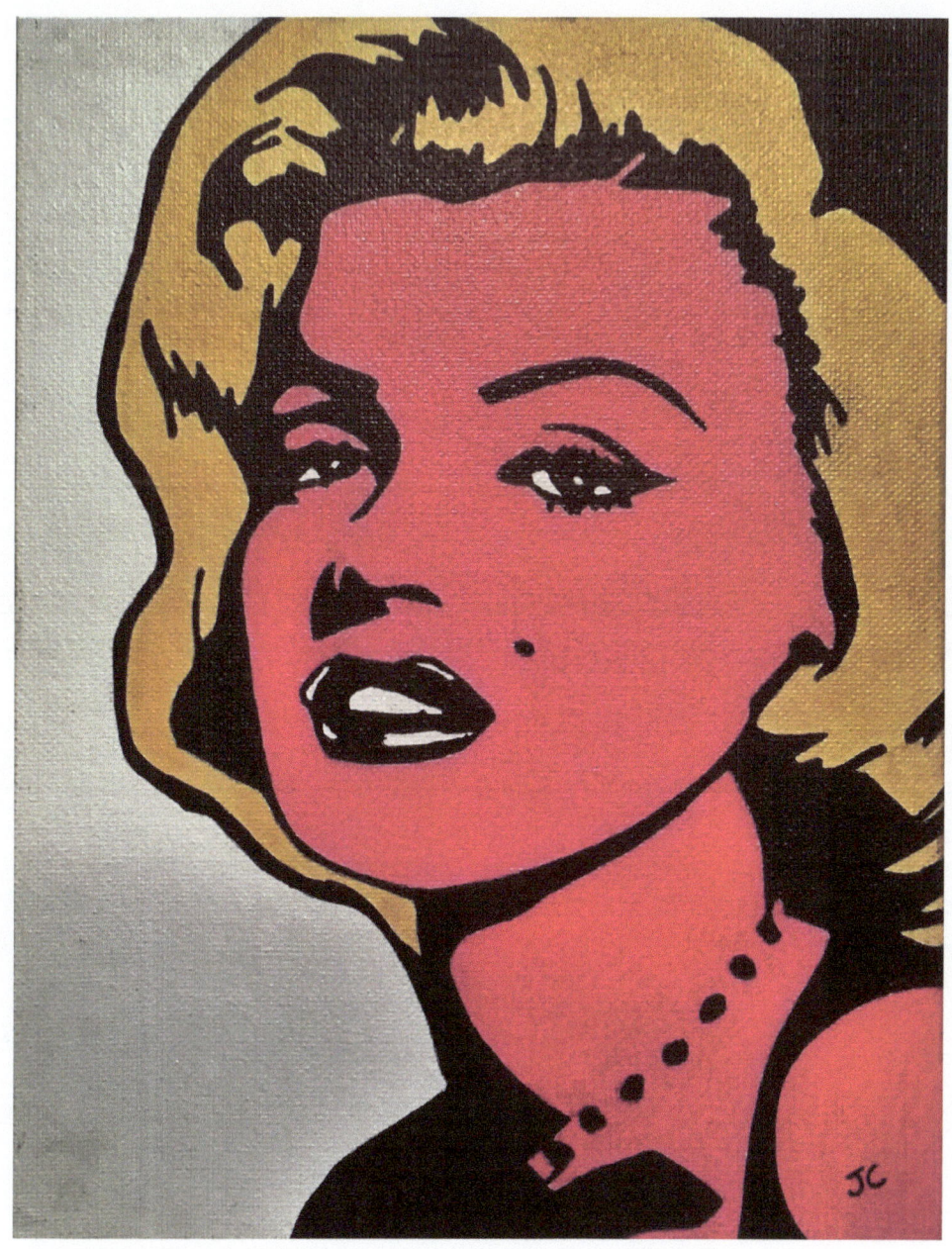

Author

Denise Fulmer has known she wanted to be an artist since the age of 3. She majored in Art at Furman University, Class of 1973, receiving the Mattie Hipp Cunningham Scholarship for Excellence in Creativity in the Visual Arts in her junior year (1972). She has worked professionally as a technical illustrator and has undertaken freelance work in painting and drawing. Her vision is romantic, whimsical, and spiritual. Also Denise has created hand-woven items for sale at craft fairs. She has created cloth dolls and stuffed animals, which were donated to local toy drives for distribution at Christmas. Denise has created 10 self-published books through Blurb.com. Five are now on Amazon.com. Four of these books on Amazon have book trailers on YouTube. Denise has created 32 videos on YouTube about her interests in art, poetry, books, animals, and family. She also has contributed to Niume, a blogging platform based in the UK, for one year before it was disbanded due to lack of funds. Her blogs were a combination of her art and writing, often using her art to illustrate her poetry. She was honored with Staff Picks for 2 out of 50 of her blogs while there.
In 2008, Denise was diagnosed with Parkinson's disease, but continues to sell her art through FineArtAmerica.com and her own website here:
https://2-denise-fulmer.pixels.com
Her Author Page on Amazon is here: amazon.com/author/denisefulmer
Denise demonstrates her courage and resilience when she explains,
"I am still an artist, no matter what condition my body is in. Being an artist is a condition of the soul."

Stars of the Silver Screen

ANNA PACQUIN – ART BY DENISE FULMER

9.0 x 12.0 inches

MEDIA - PASTEL ON PAPER

$50.00

dffladybug@gmail.com

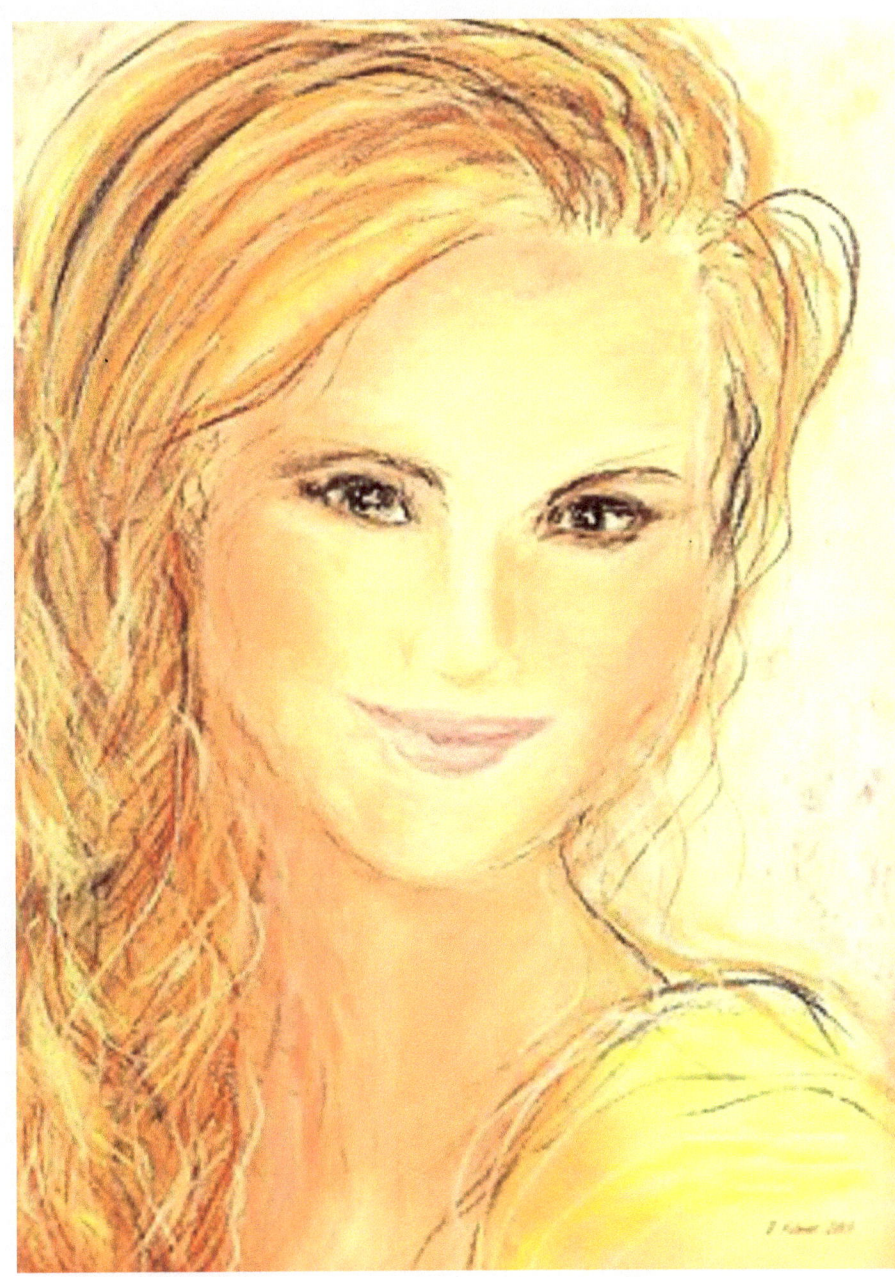

VERONICA LAKE – ART BY DENISE FULMER

9.0 x 11.5 inches

MEDIA - PENCIL, CHARCOAL ON PAPER

$50.00

dffladybug@gmail.com

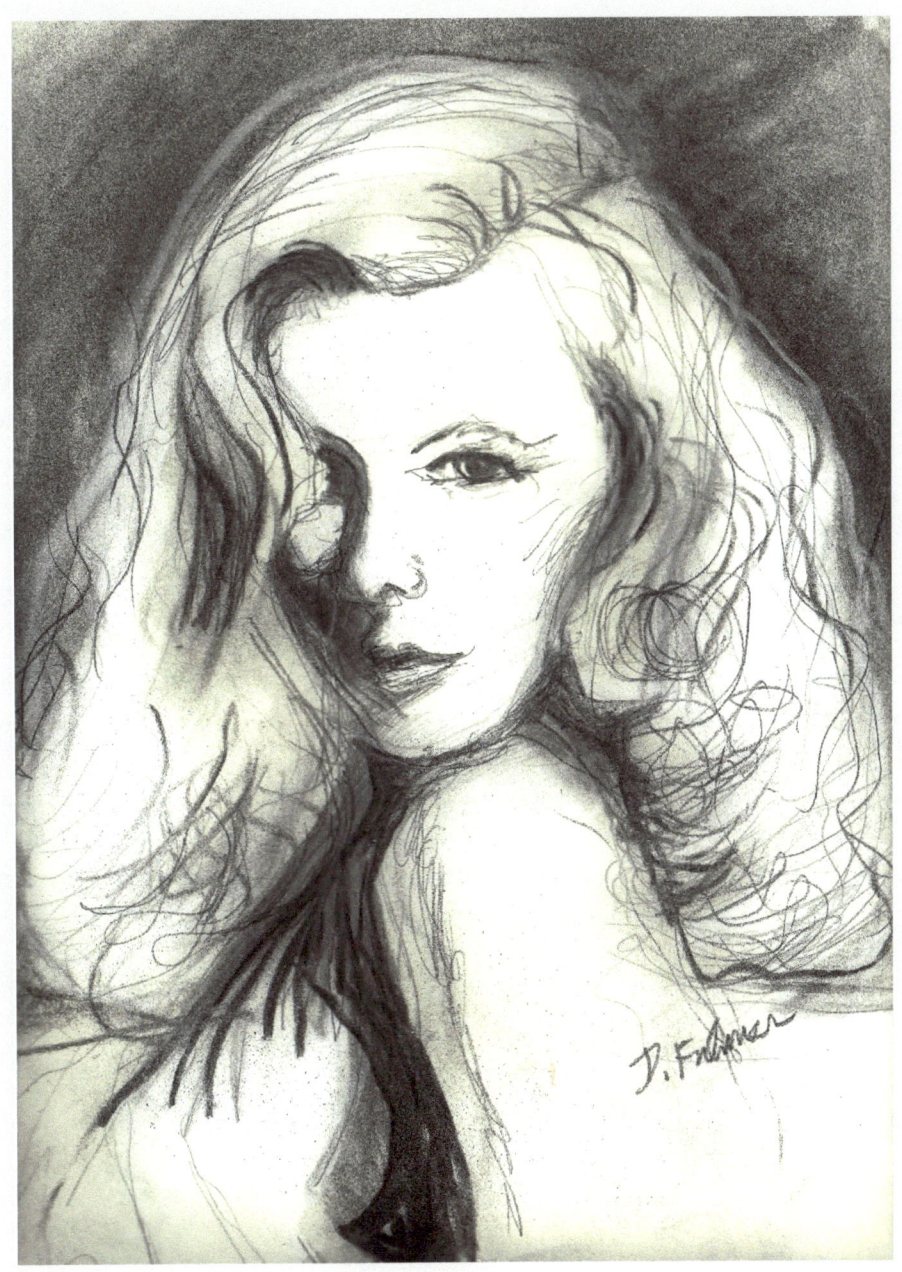

Author

Ramesh Mahalingam has had a lifelong passion for art - it runs in the family - from his grandfather to his aunt, sister and cousins, passion for the arts has been a common thread running through the family.

Ramesh has a Master's degree from the University of Michigan.. He worked in Pepsi-Co Inc. in the USA for 15 years in various levels. He then returned back to India - to his roots. In India he set up a packaging manufacturing unit. Now retired, he now has the time to devote to his passion – painting.

Ramesh did not have a formal education in arts. He is basically self -taught. Just watching other artists and their works of art has inspired Ramesh to teach himself the basic concepts and techniques used by professional artists.

Ramesh has successfully conducted several exhibitions of his paintings, along with his sister Rama Balakrishnan. The exhibitions were grand successes. The proceeds of the sale of paintings at the exhibitions were donated to charity.

Ramesh dabbles in all art forms, acrylic, watercolors, pencil sketches as well as multi-media works. All of these came out of his personal interest and passion in the field.

Stars of the Silver Screen

MANISHA KOIRALA – ART BY RAMESH MAHALINGHAM

16.0 x 20.0 inches

MEDIA - ACRYLICS

$100.00

rxm1951@gmail.com

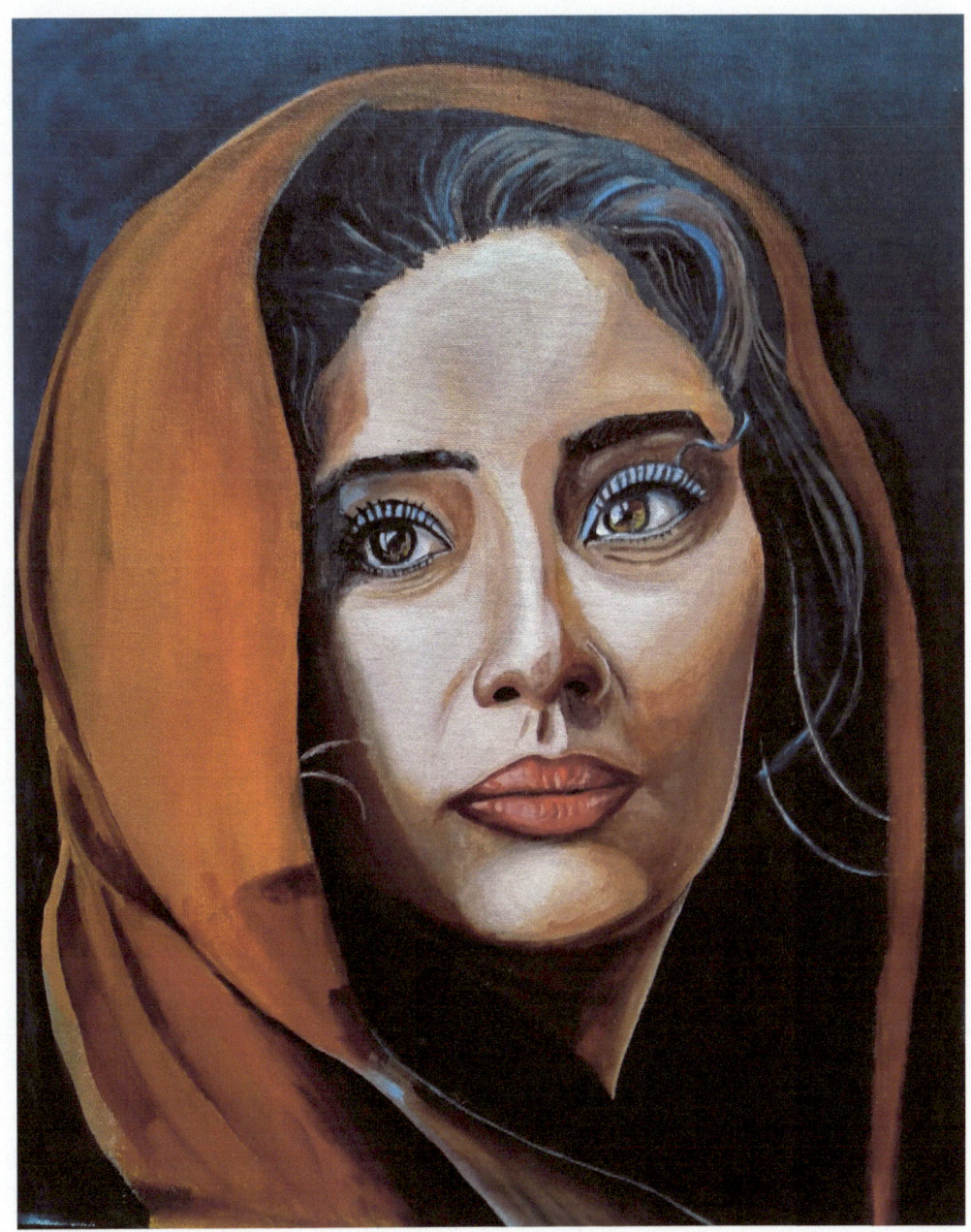

ABOUT THE AUTHOR

At the age of 15, he started to write short stories, poems, screen plays. When 19 of age, worked as technician at the film studios, department for special effects and light. Worked also on movie Amadeus, directed by Oscar - winning director, Milos Forman. At age 24, emigrated to United States. In 1989 moved to California where he joined theatre group Gilbert & Sullivan. During his stay in California went to Santa Barbara Community College where he visited several accredited courses as Business law and Design. After death of his father in 2001, he returned to his birth country where he worked as Quality Engineer, Quality Assurance manager and Manufacturing Project Manager. In quality assurance he got Black Belt / 6 Sigma training while working in automotive industry. He had few art shows in Europe and United States. On top of fine art painting, he also started to do sculptures and the other strong activity that he spent a lot of time with design inventions, technical and design improvements in fields like optics, acoustics and motion picture E^2E^2 systems. Currently he writes his first screenplay for a film which he is going to direct it too.

E MAIL CONTACT: motyl_1999@yahoo.com

Stars of the Silver Screen

www.ingramcontent.com/pod-product-compliance
Lightning Source LLC
Chambersburg PA
CBHW051219220526
45473CB00003B/1092